JPBOND's

Damsel In Distress

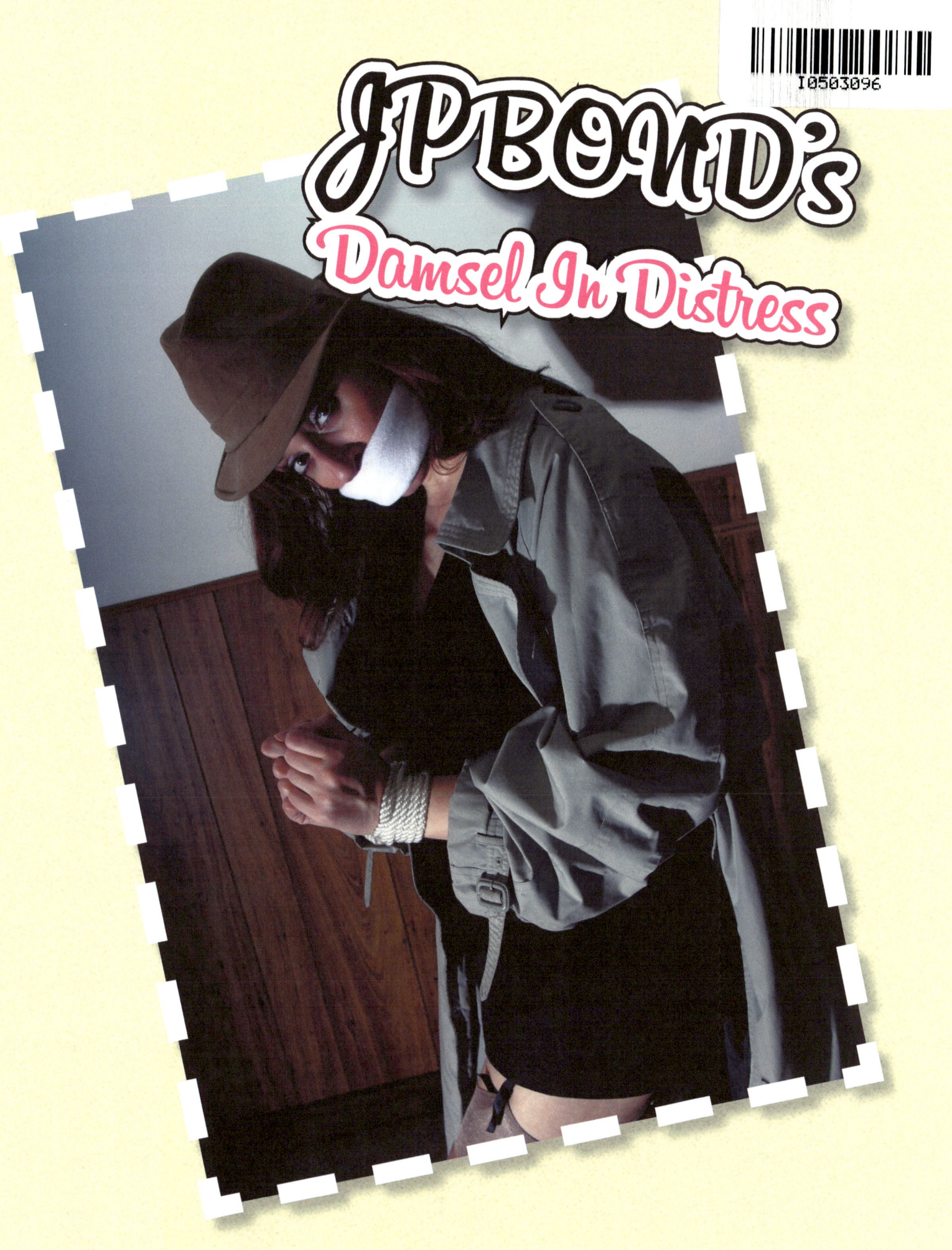

To order additional copies of this book, contact:
Xlibris Corporation
1-888-795-4274
www.Xlibris.com
Orders@Xlibris.com

I always loved pictures of damsel in distress. The old detective magazine with the cover of a woman in danger had always intrigued me. A lot of my photography goes toward that style of picture. I wanted to create that style with a story behind it. I always wanted to share my pictures with others. I hope you enjoy the book.

I dedicate this book to all the models that I had the privilege to work with over the years. Thank you for bringing your sense of style and beauty to all of my pictures. I would like to thank Tia Tormen who always inspired me to do more. I would also like to thank Dave Duzinski for helping me with editing ideas.

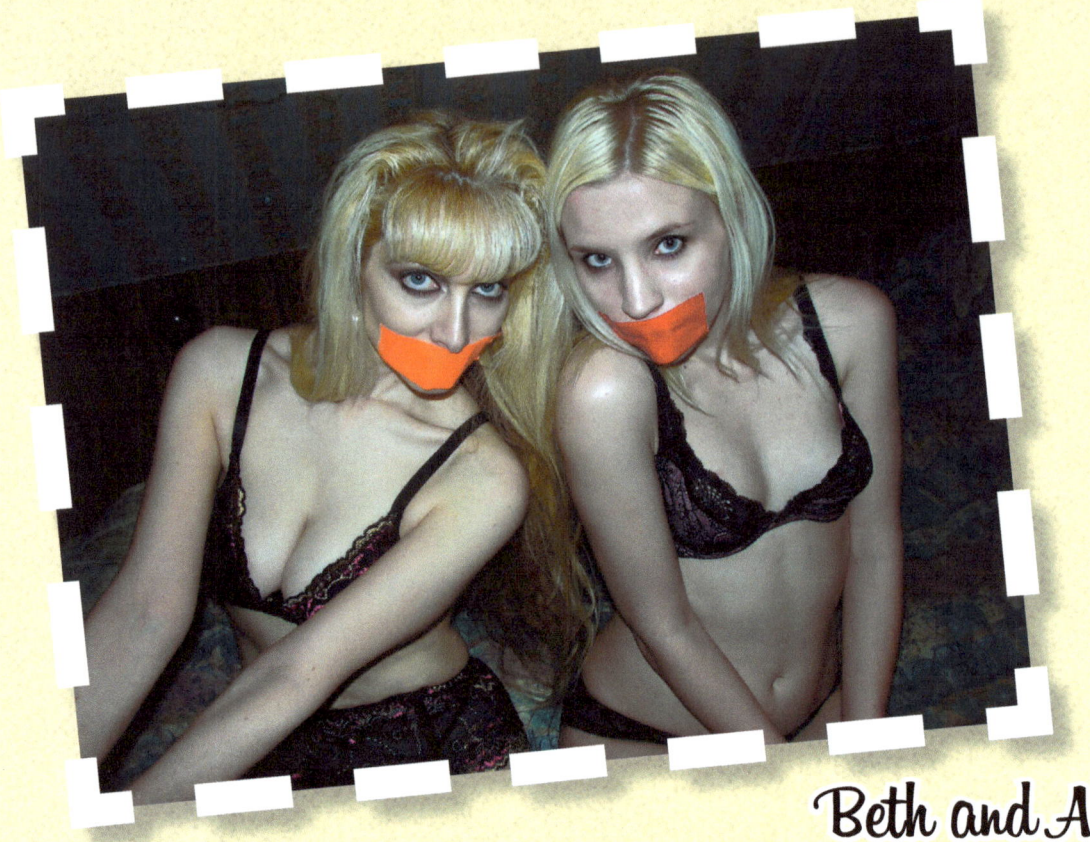

Beth and Amaya

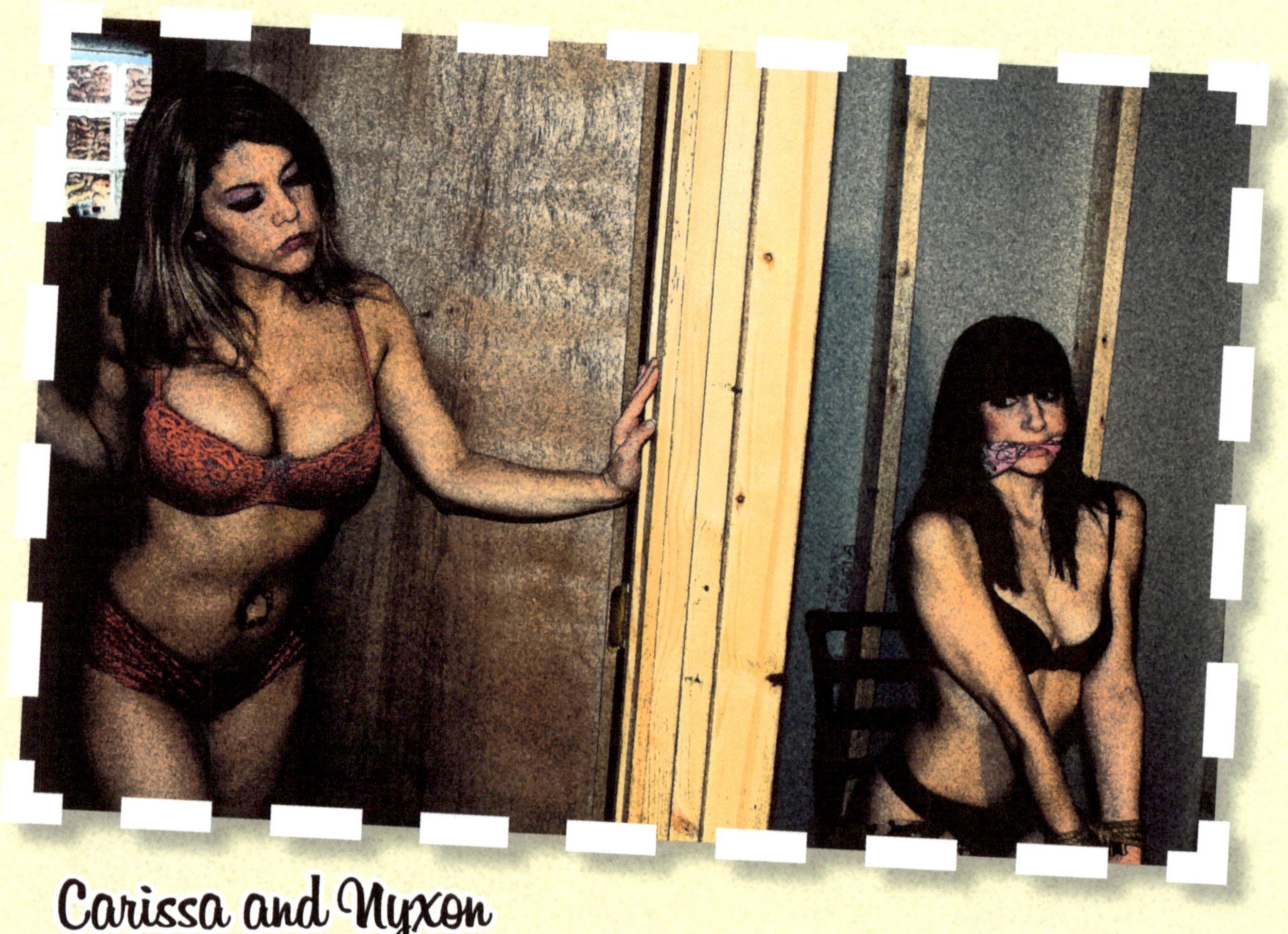

Carissa and Nyxon

4

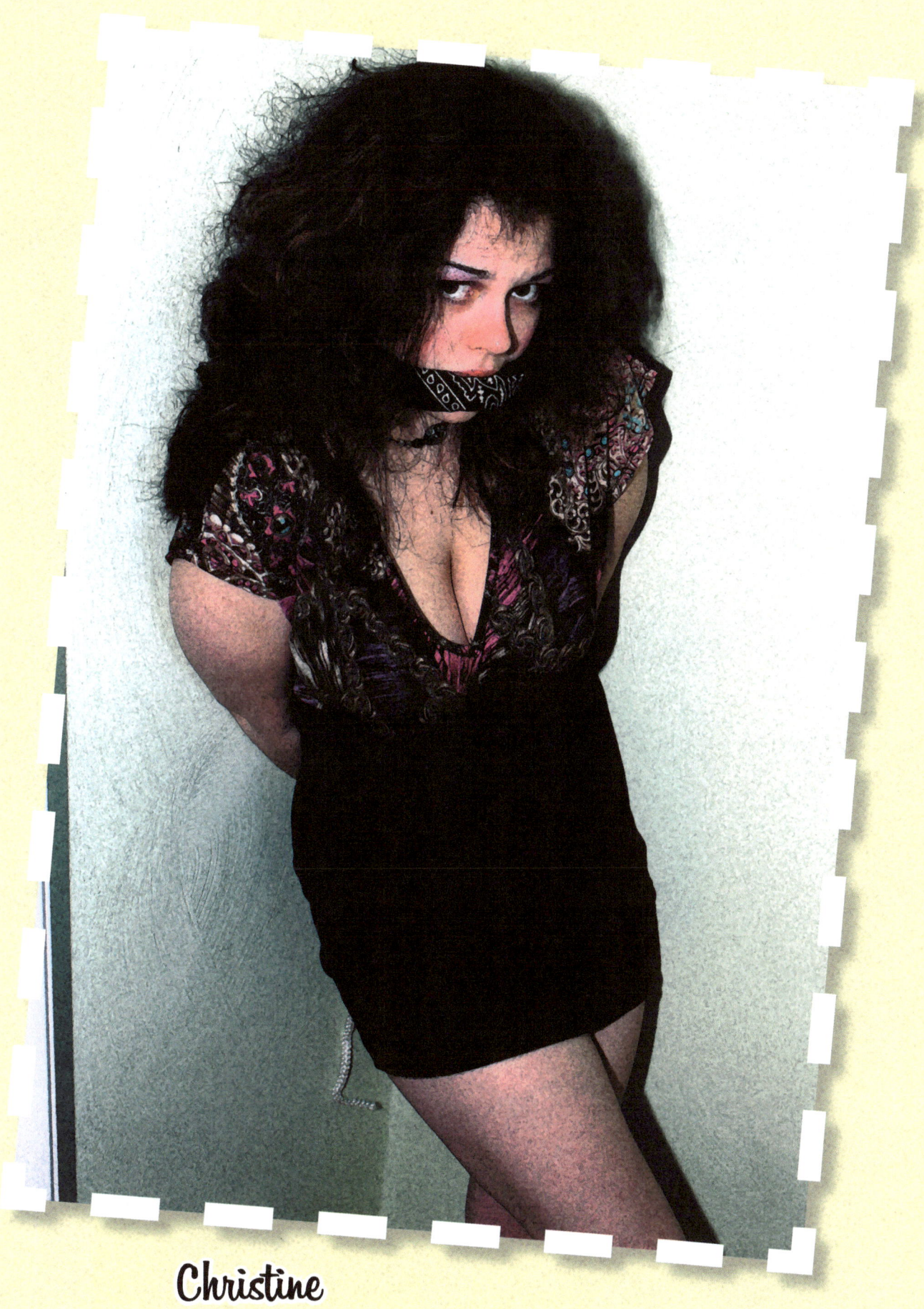

Christine

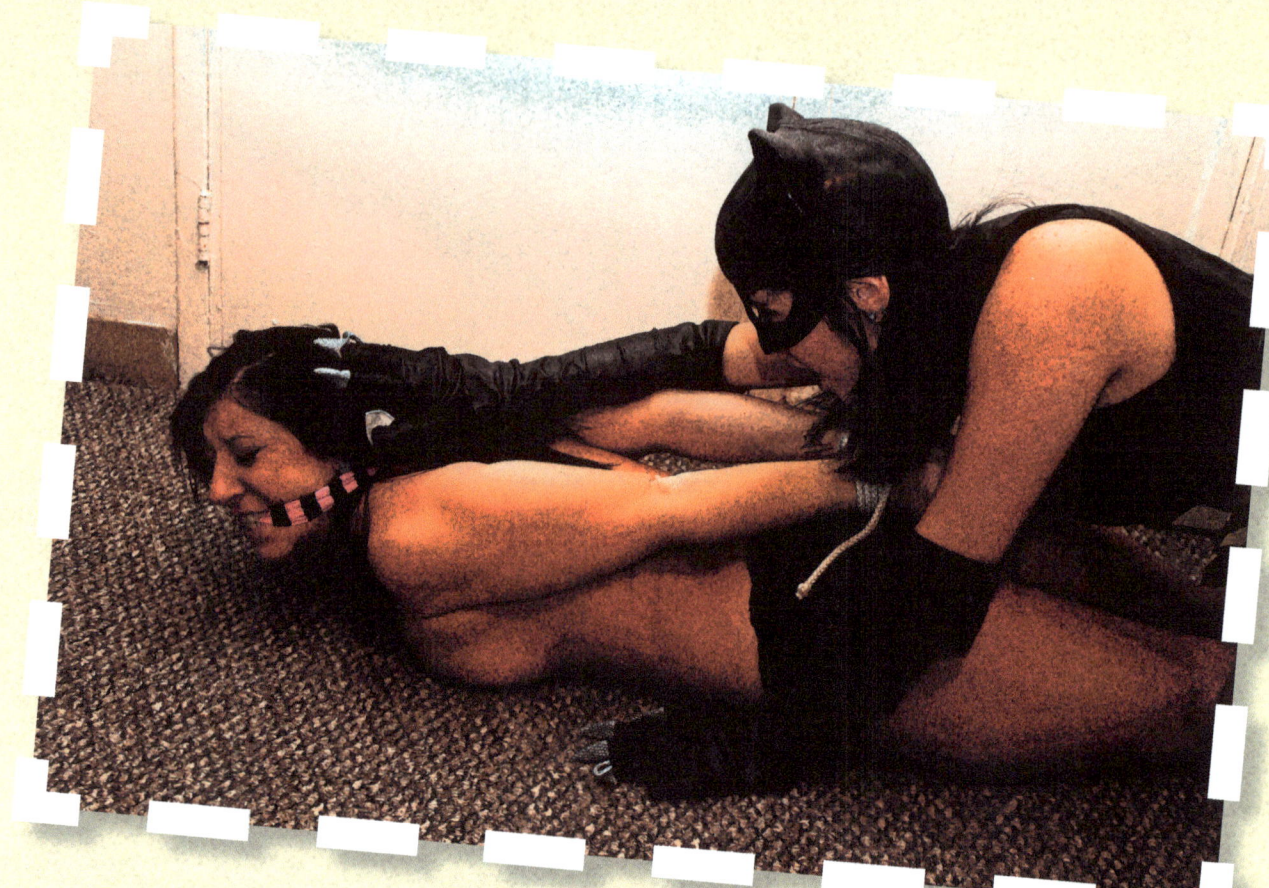

Crystal Frost and Dixie Comet

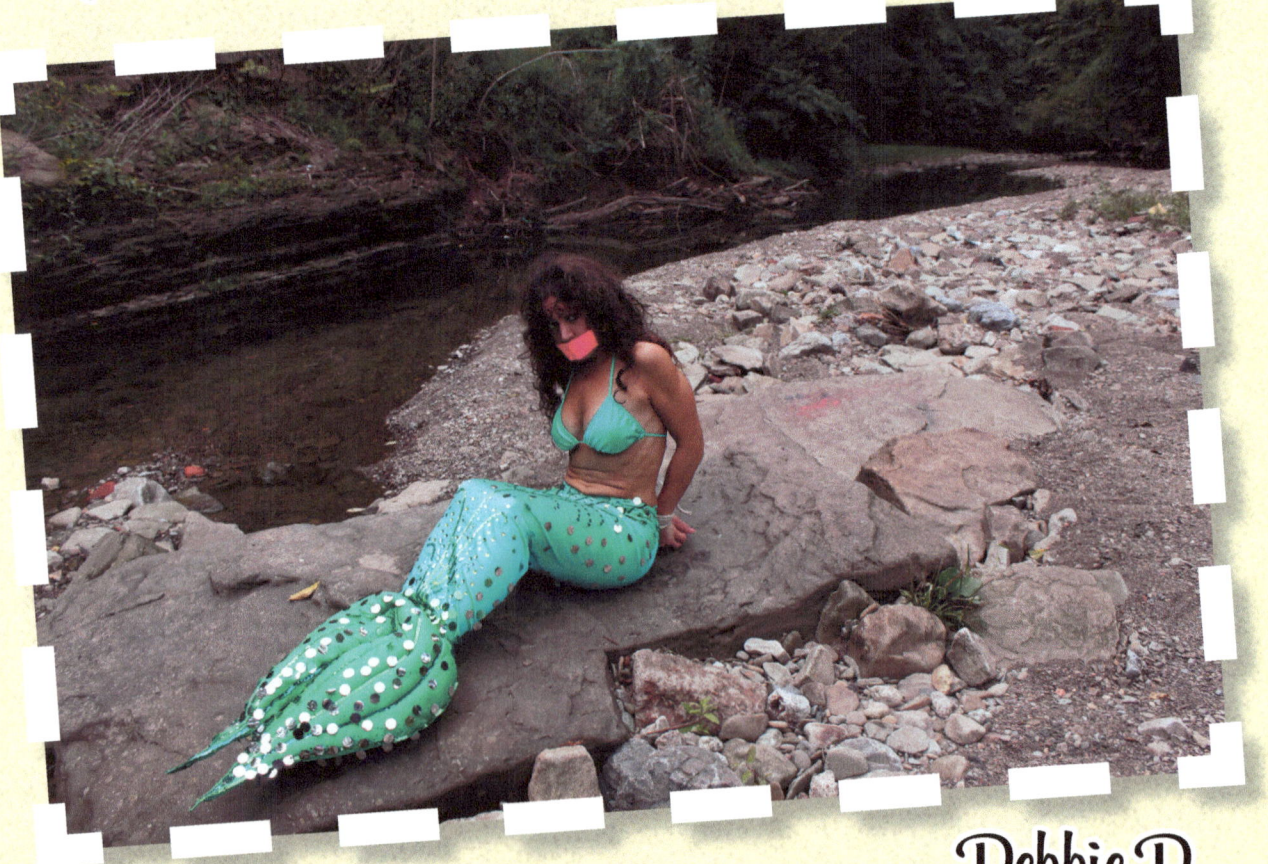

Debbie D

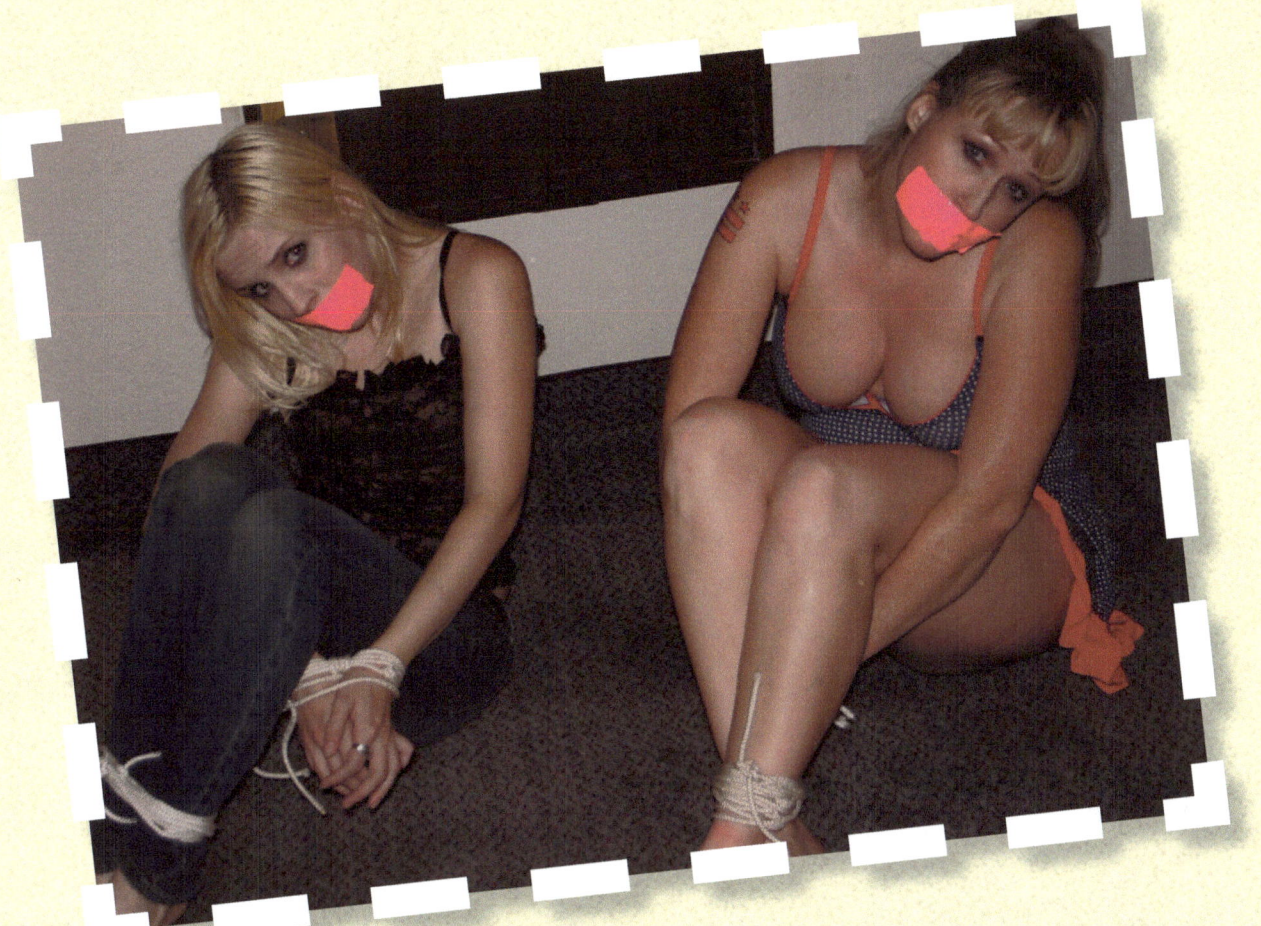

Amaya and Julie Simone

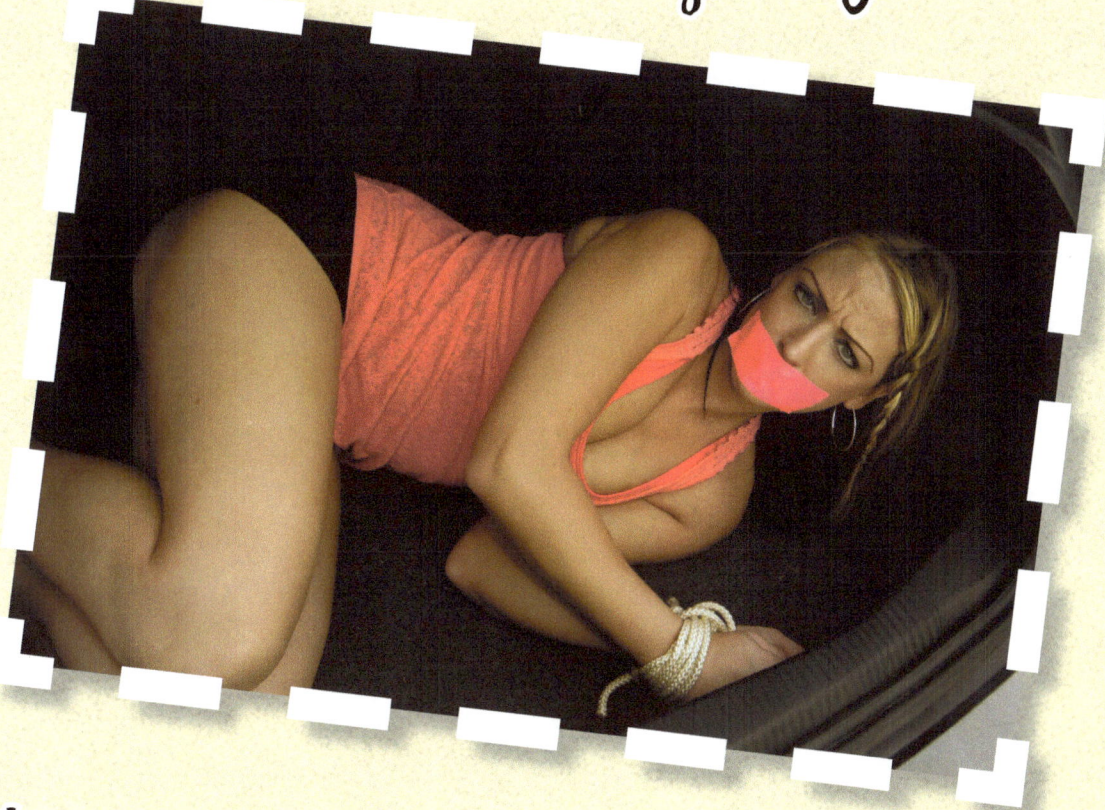

Faith

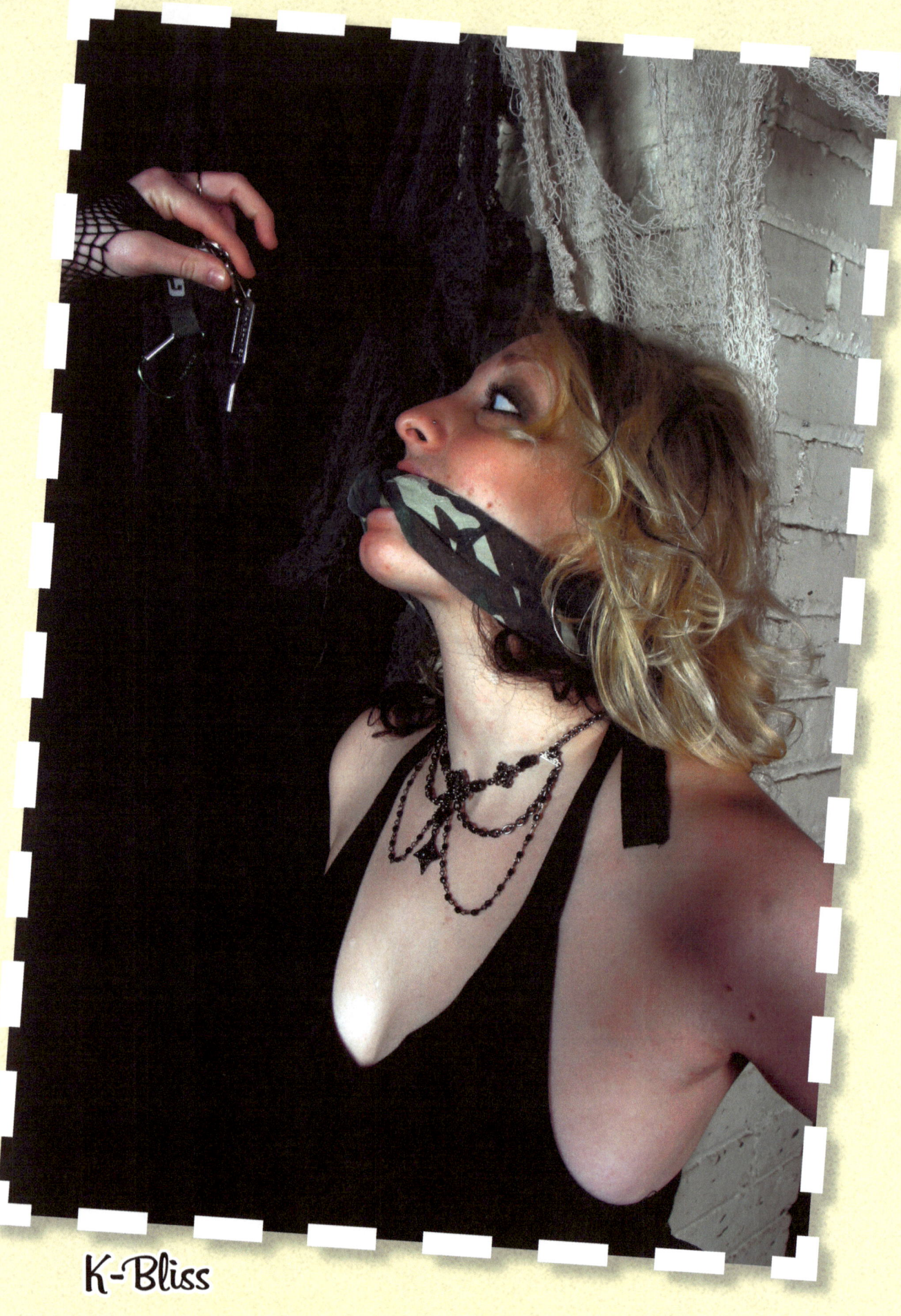

K-Bliss

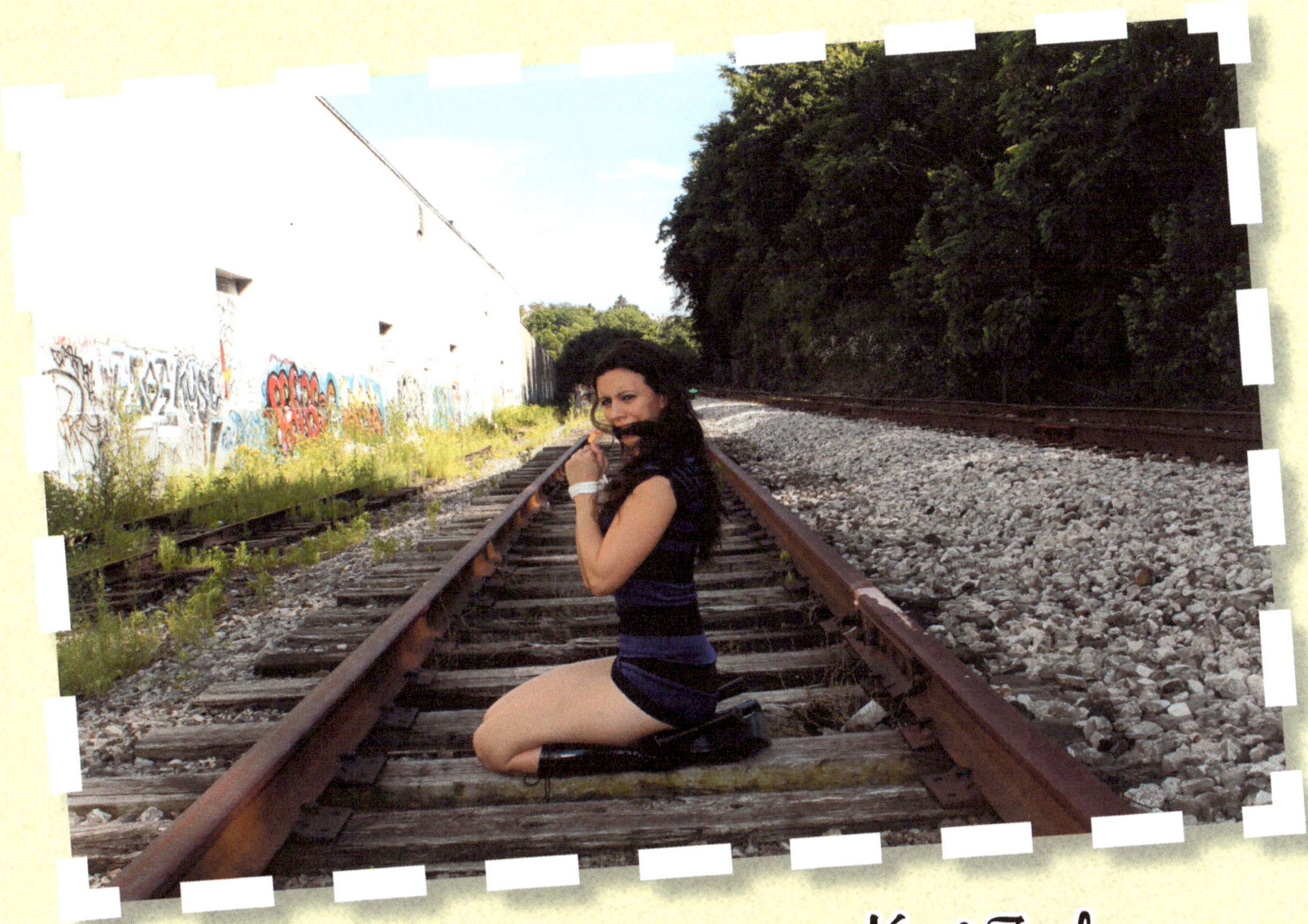

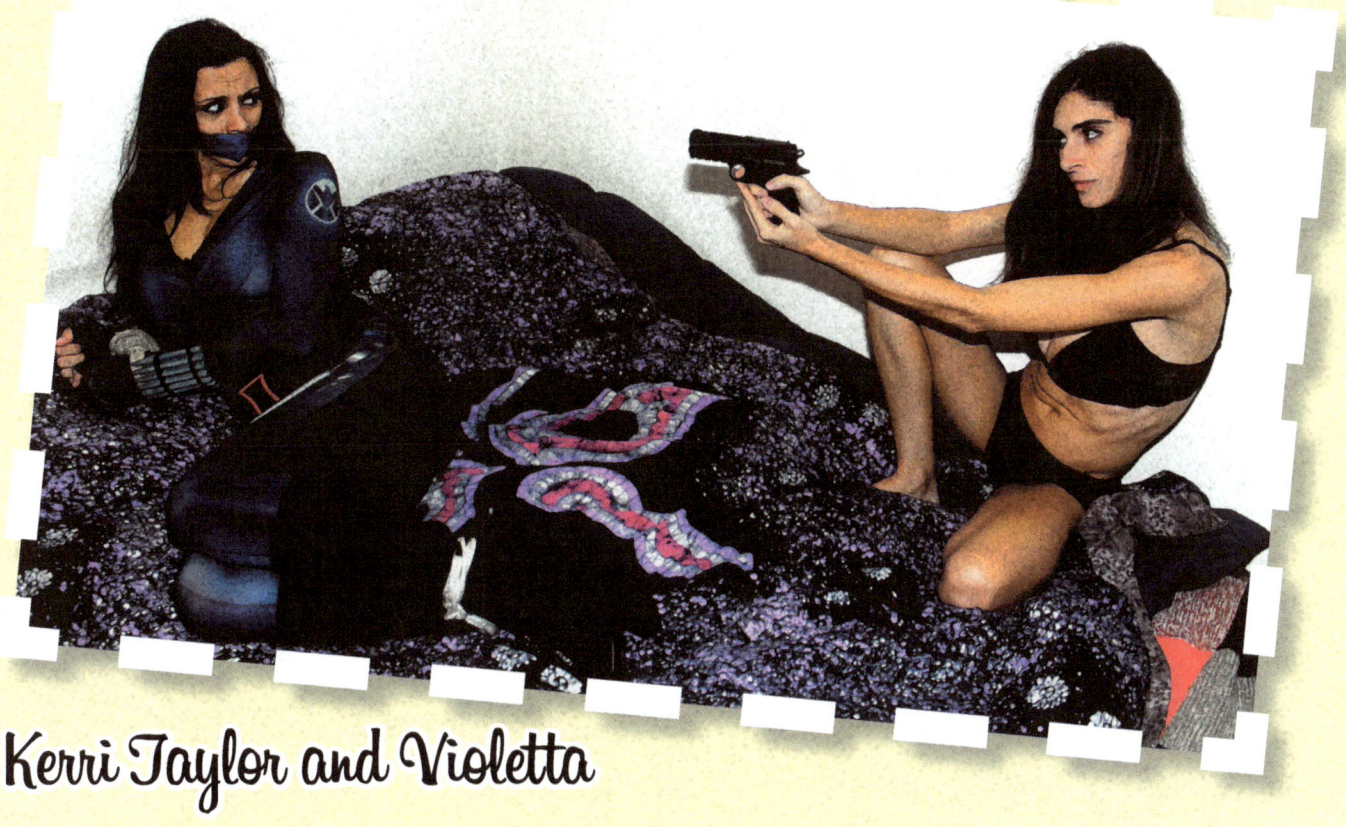

Kerri Taylor

Kerri Taylor and Violetta

9

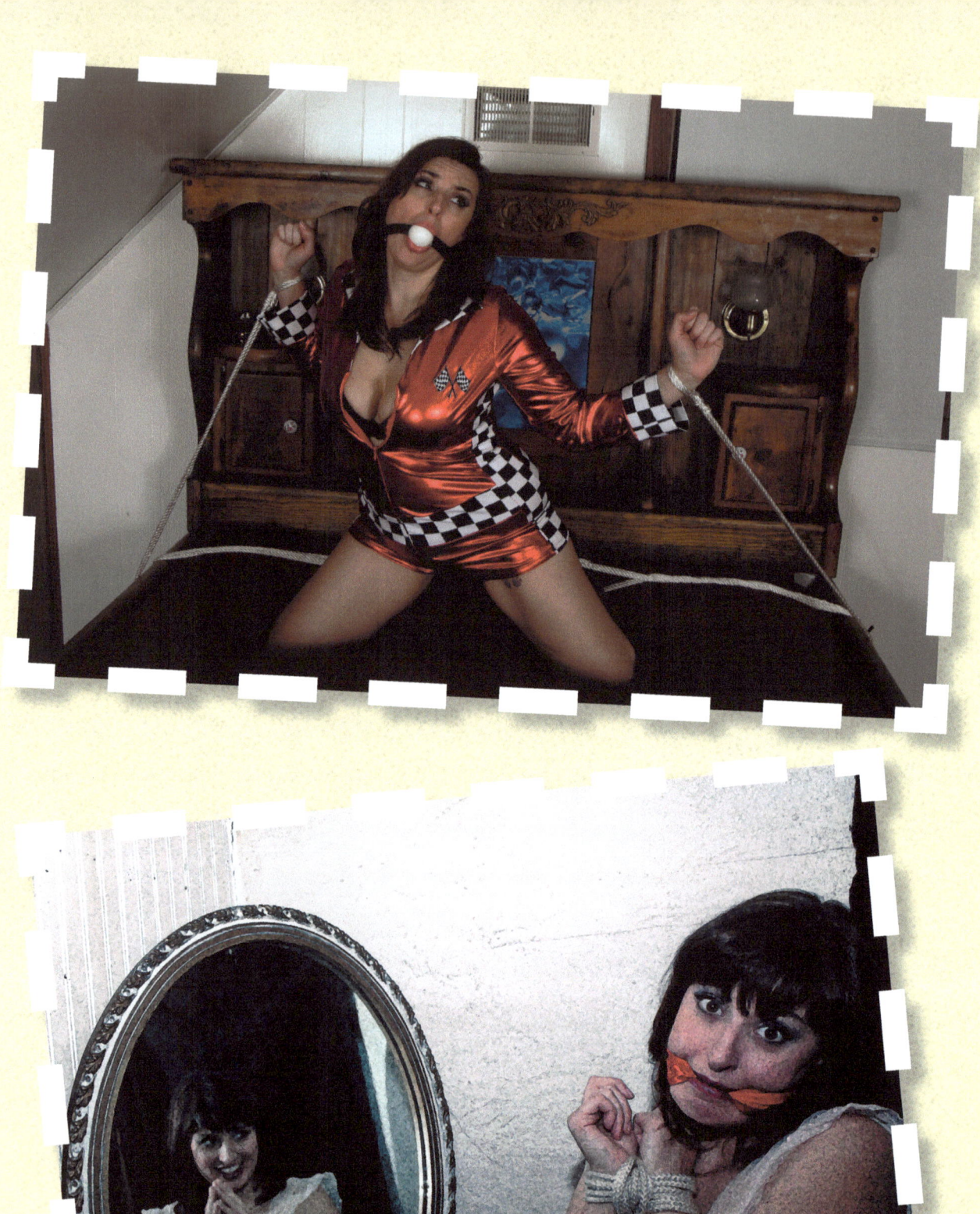

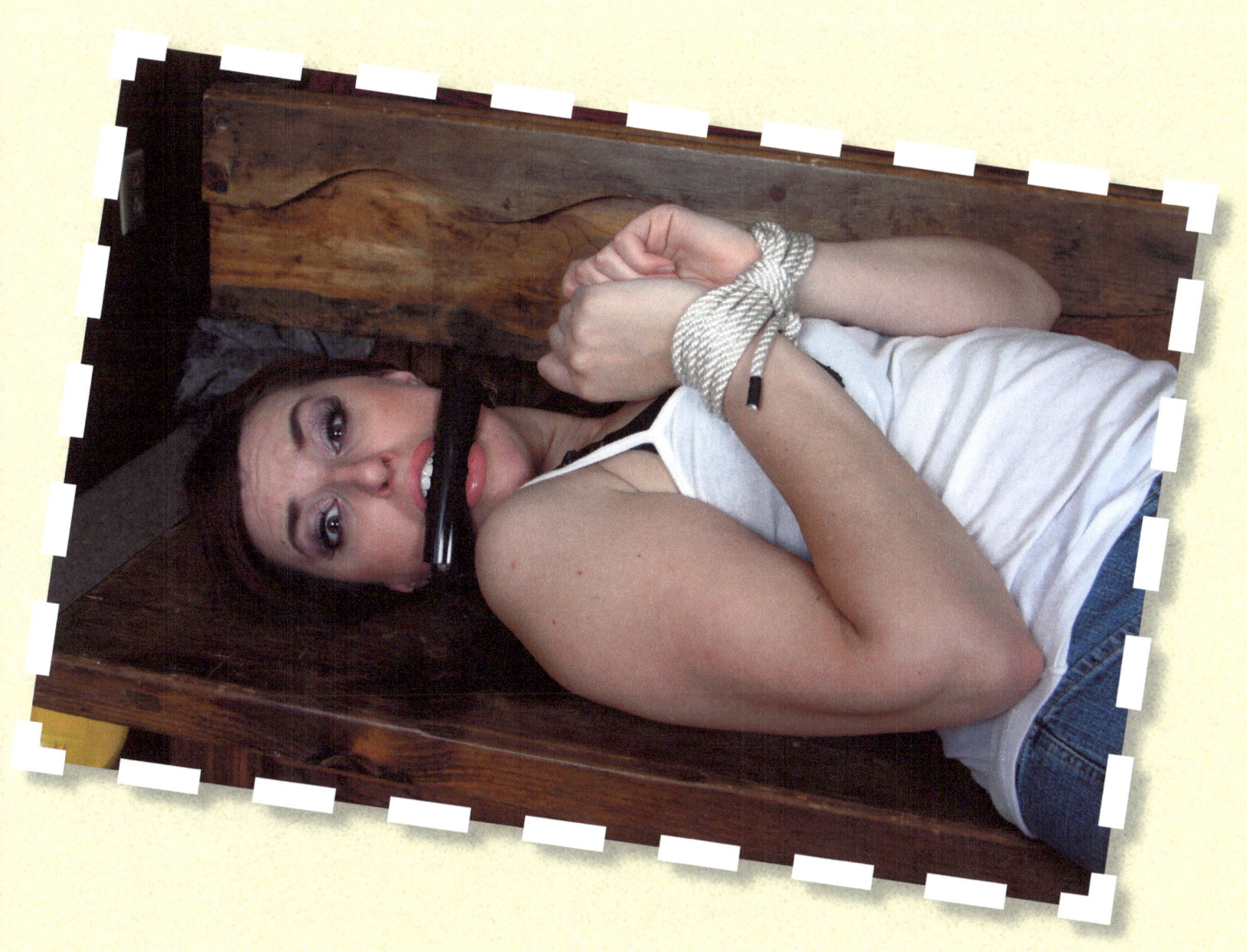

Kim Marvel

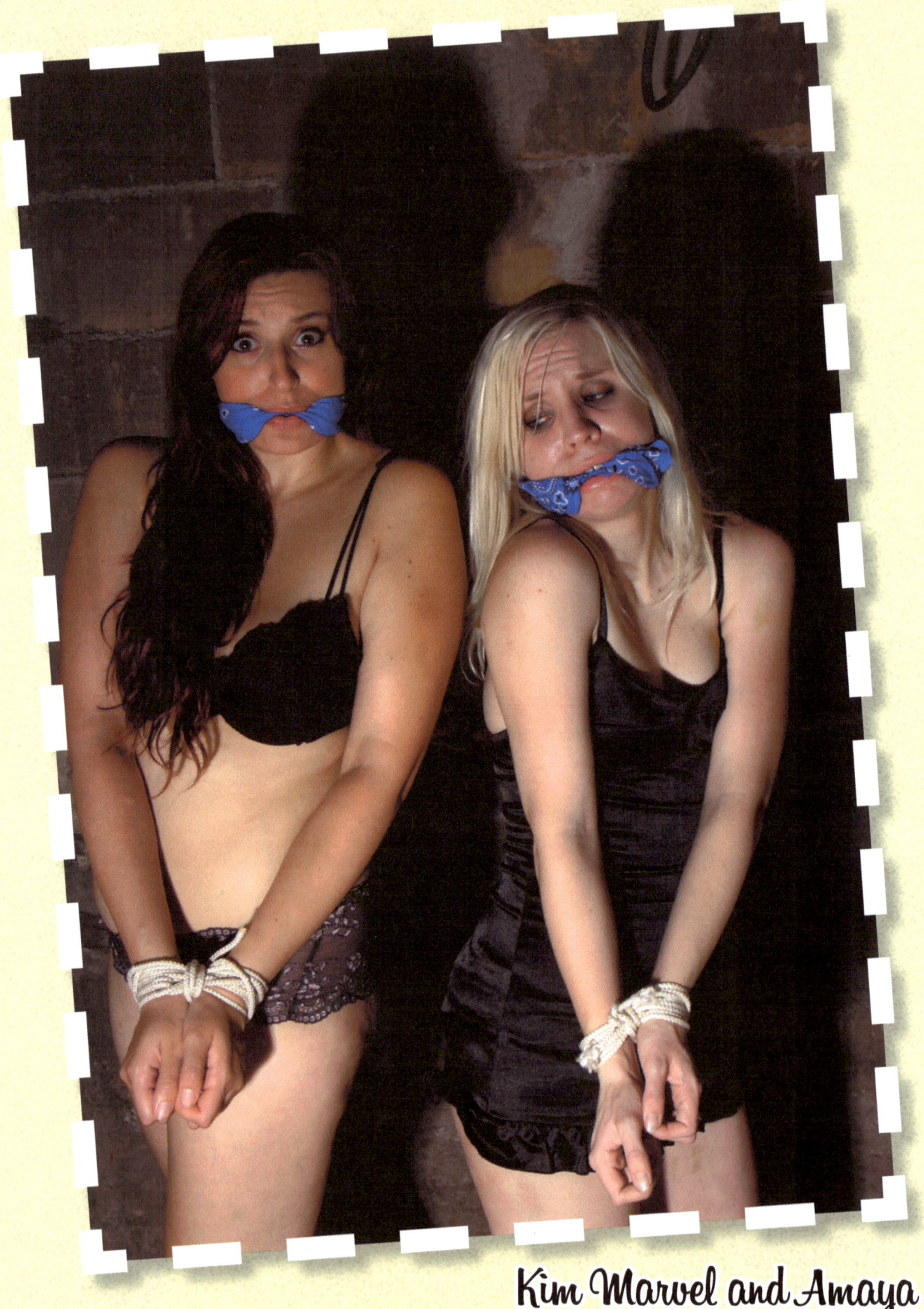

Kim Marvel and Amaya

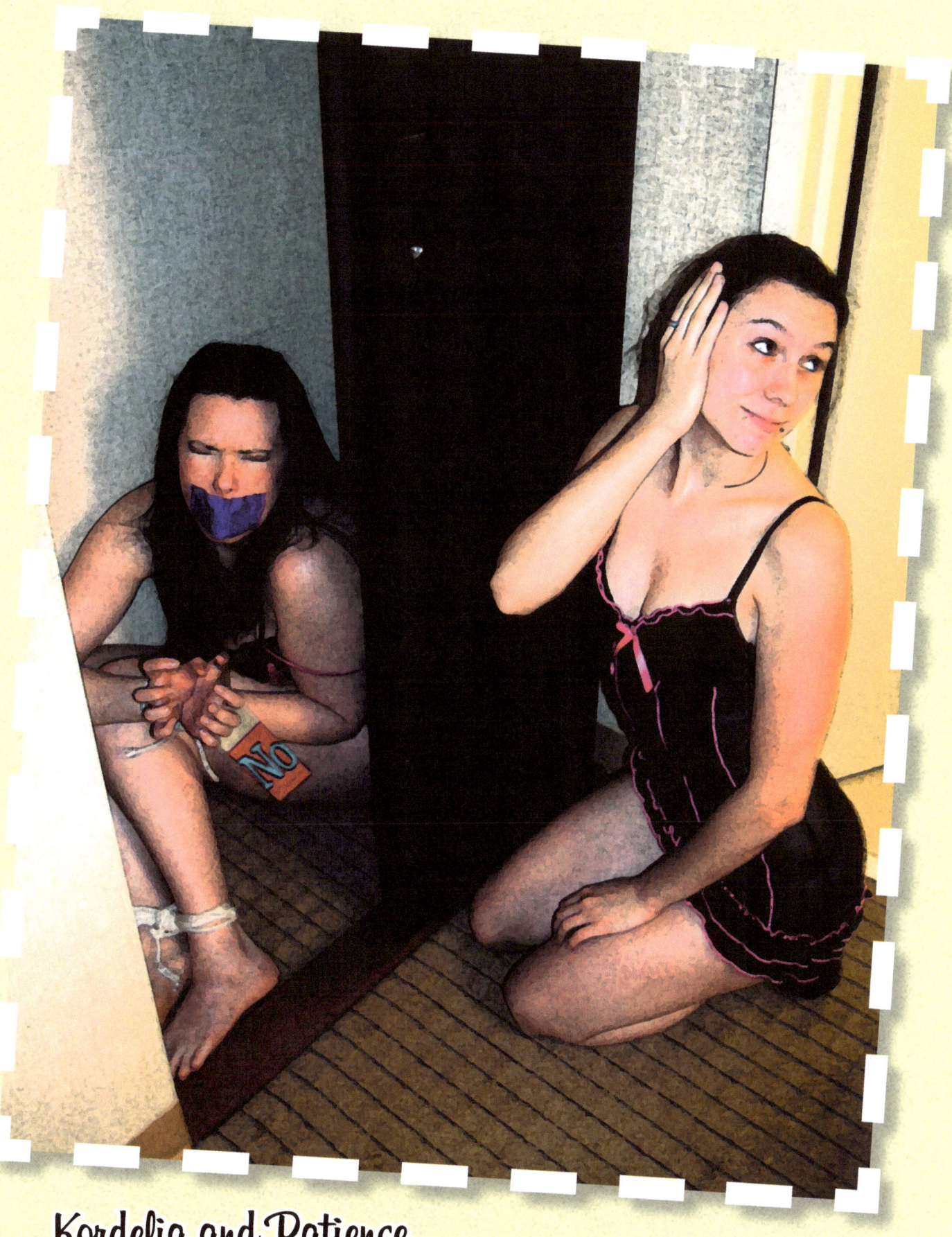

Kordelia and Patience

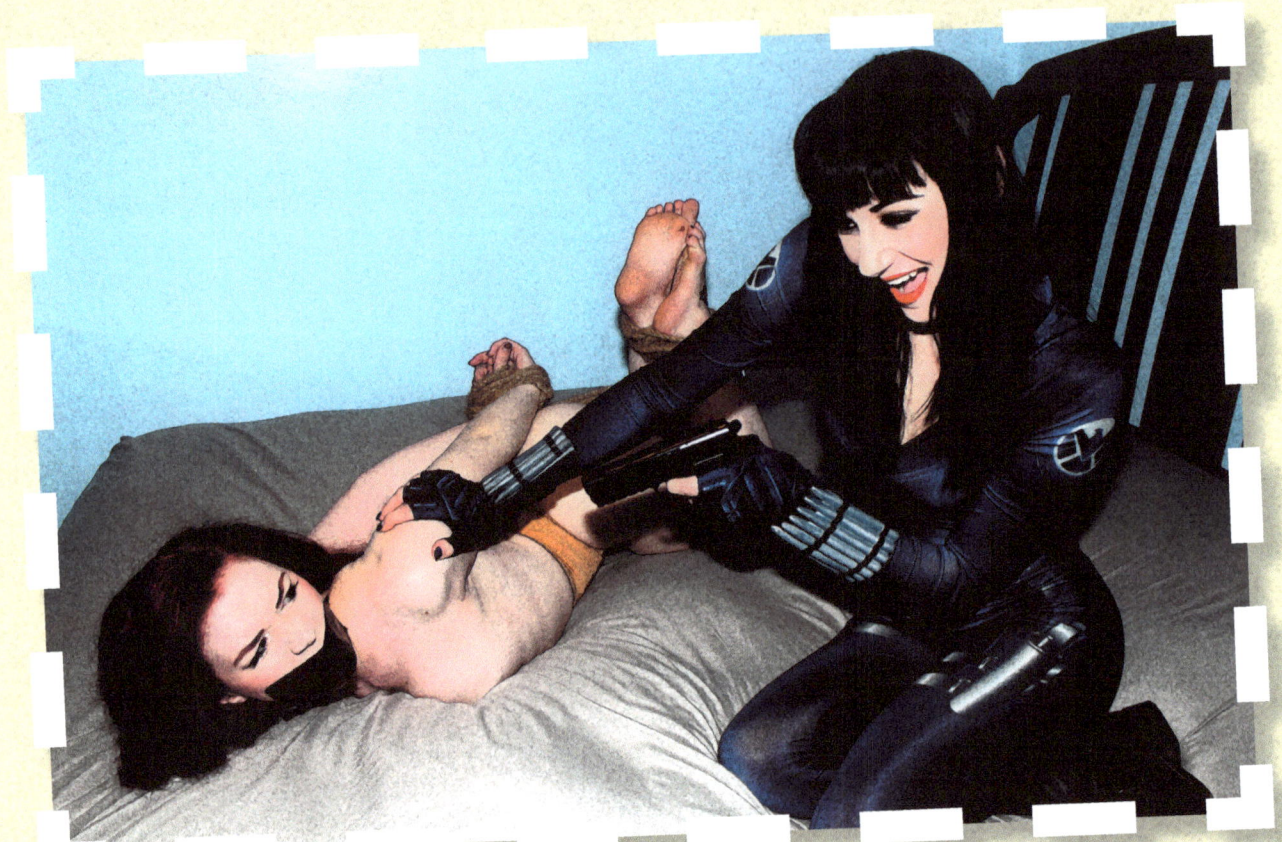

Ludella and Nyxon

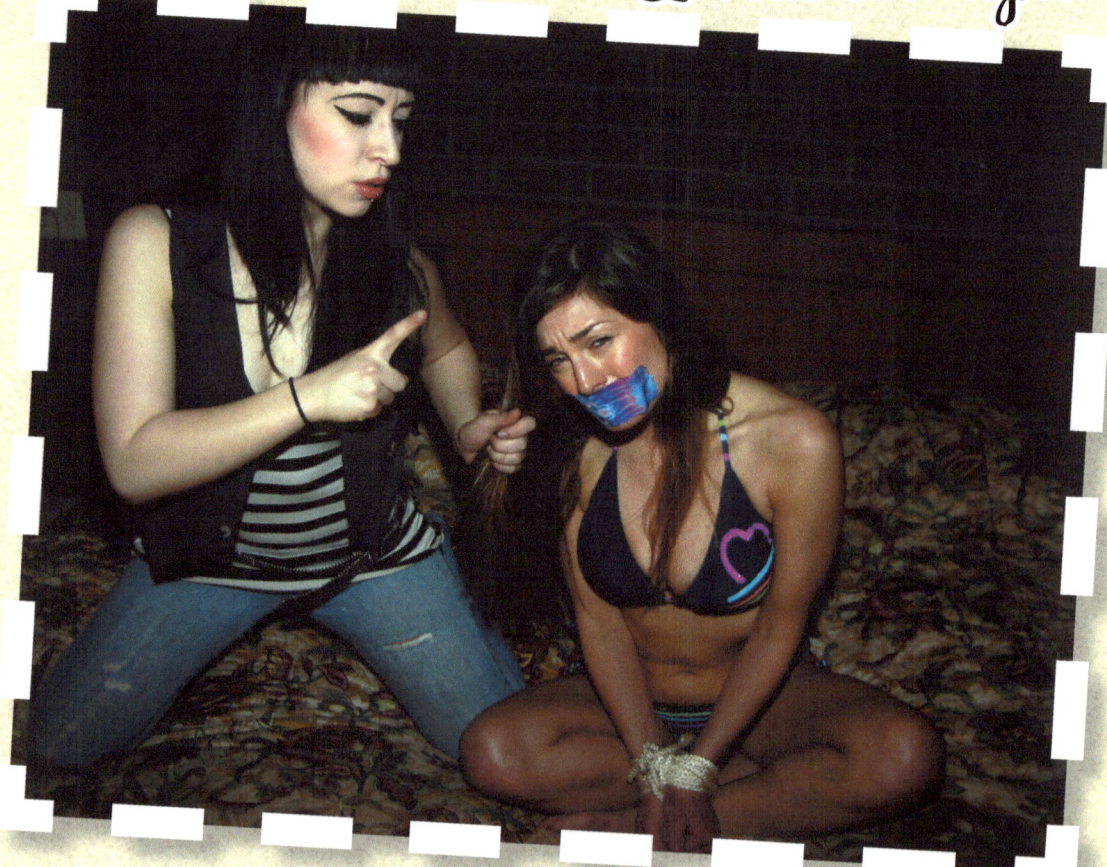

Lydia and Mia

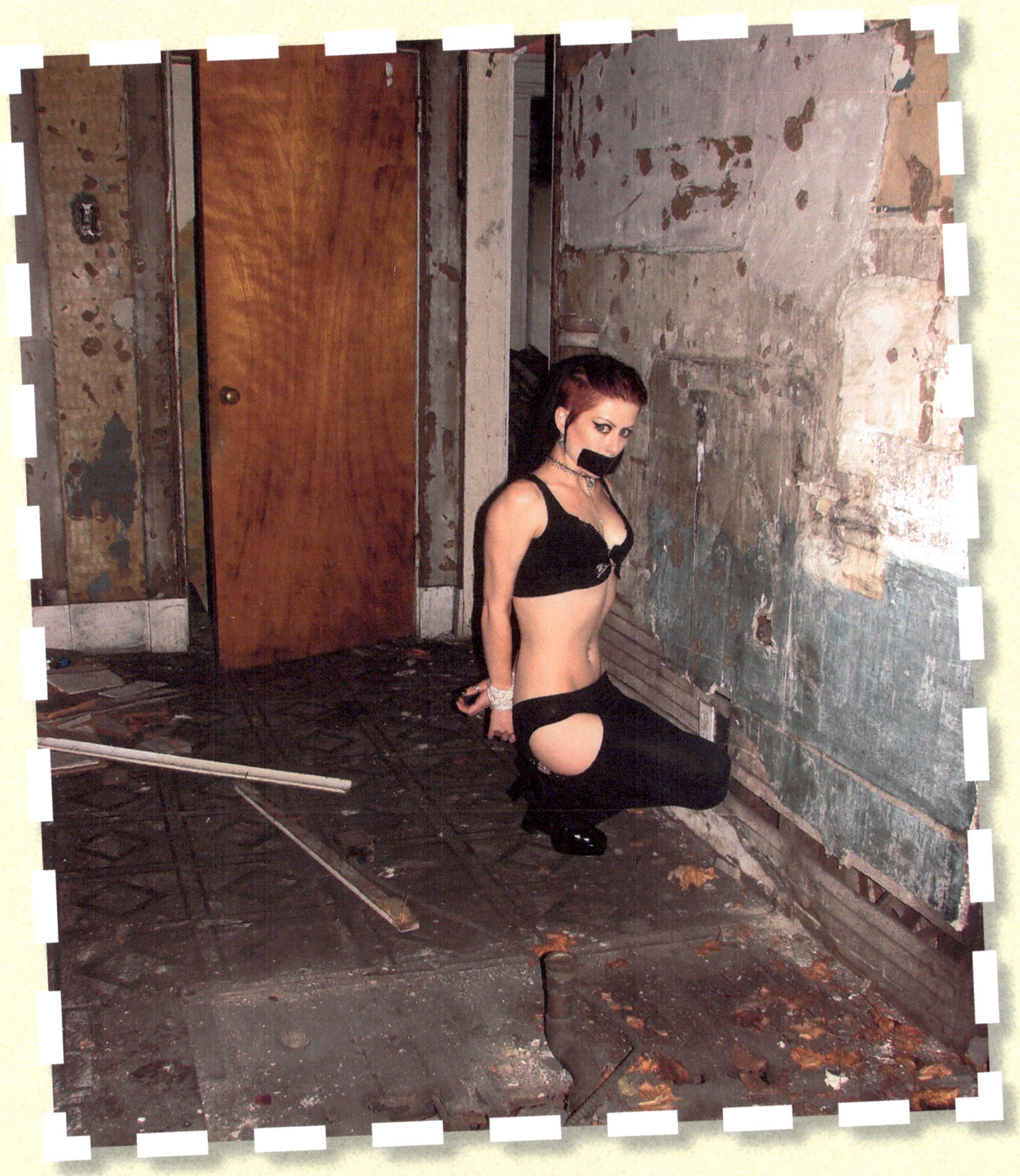

Medicine Witch

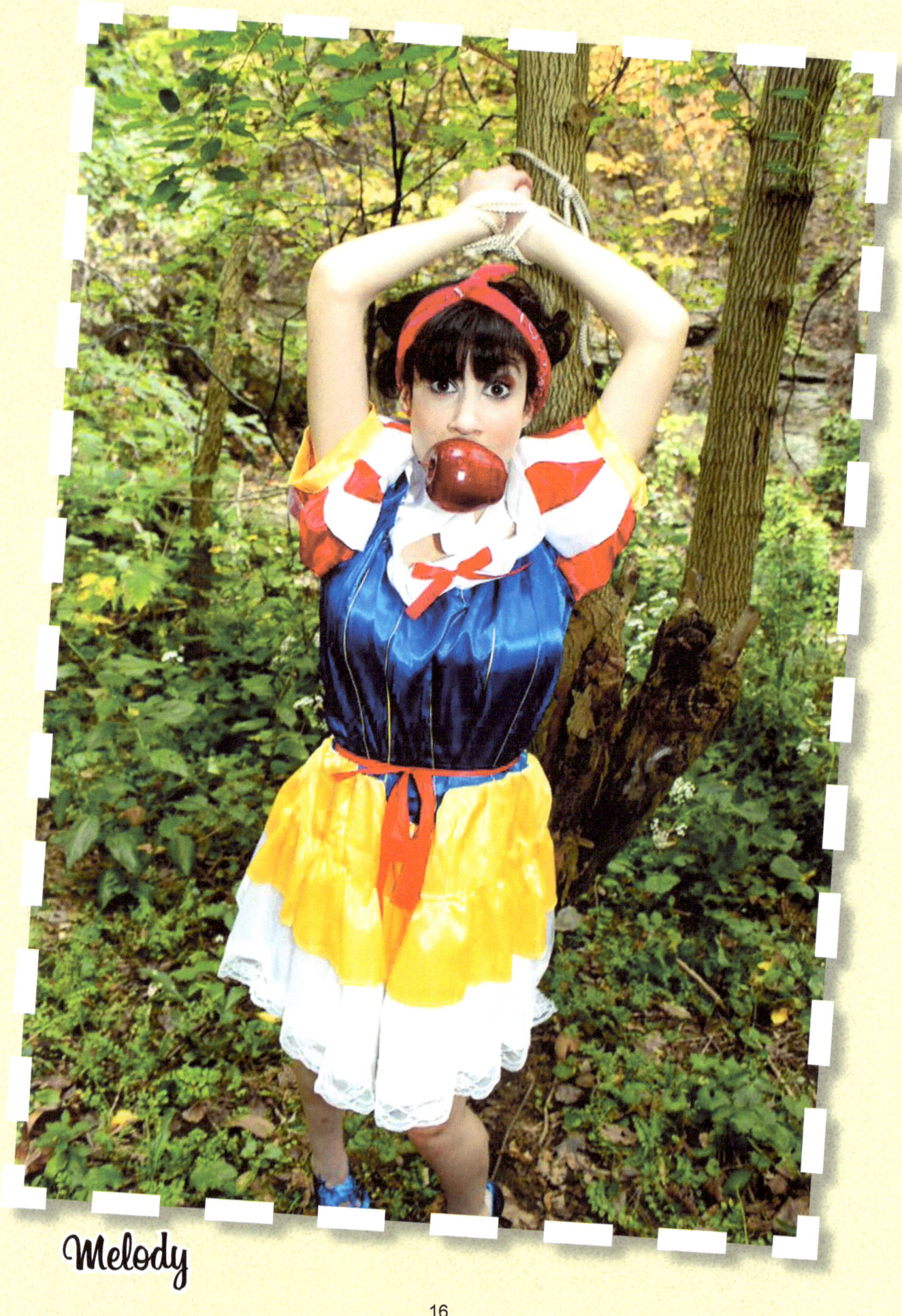

Melody

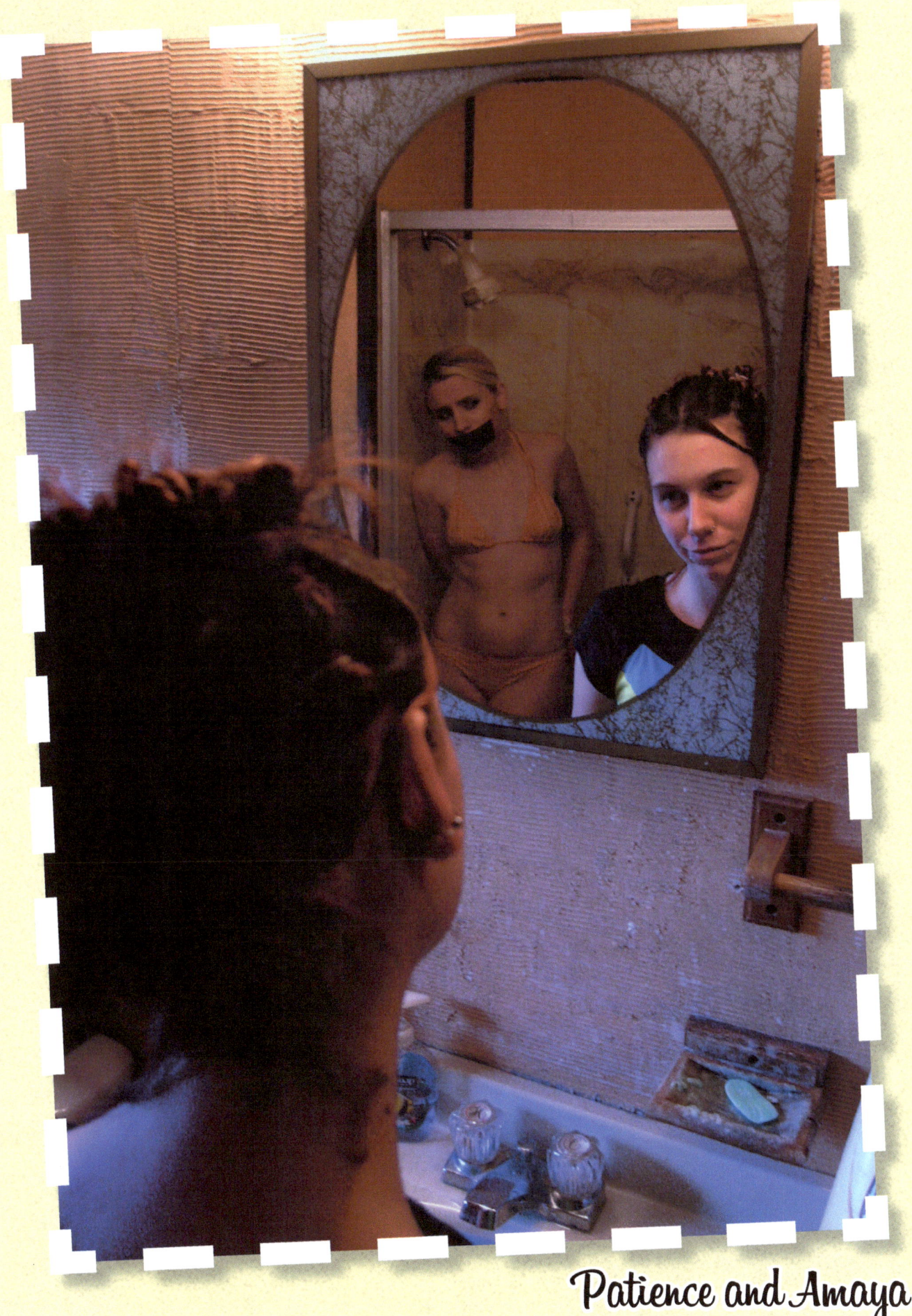

Patience and Amaya

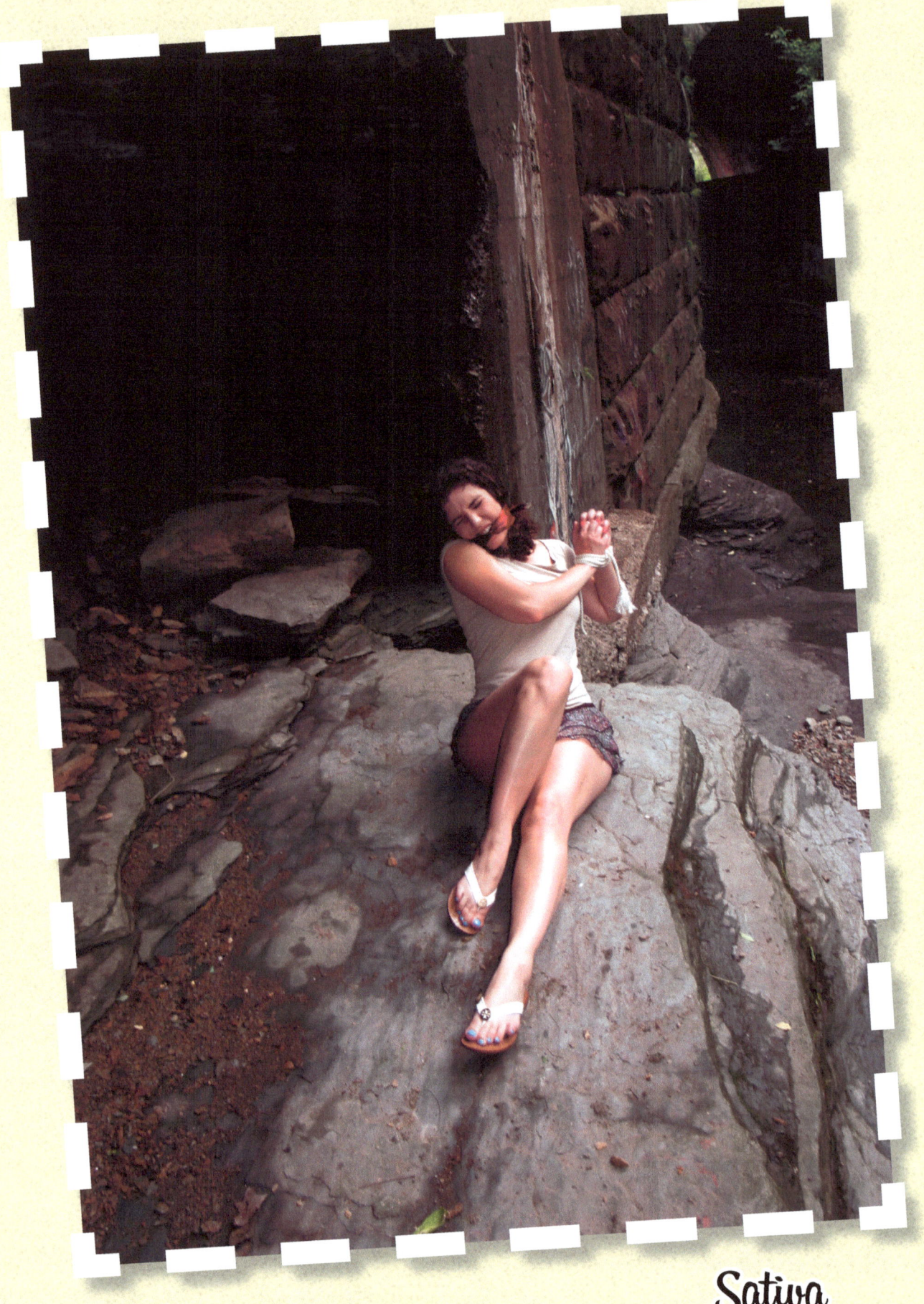

Sativa

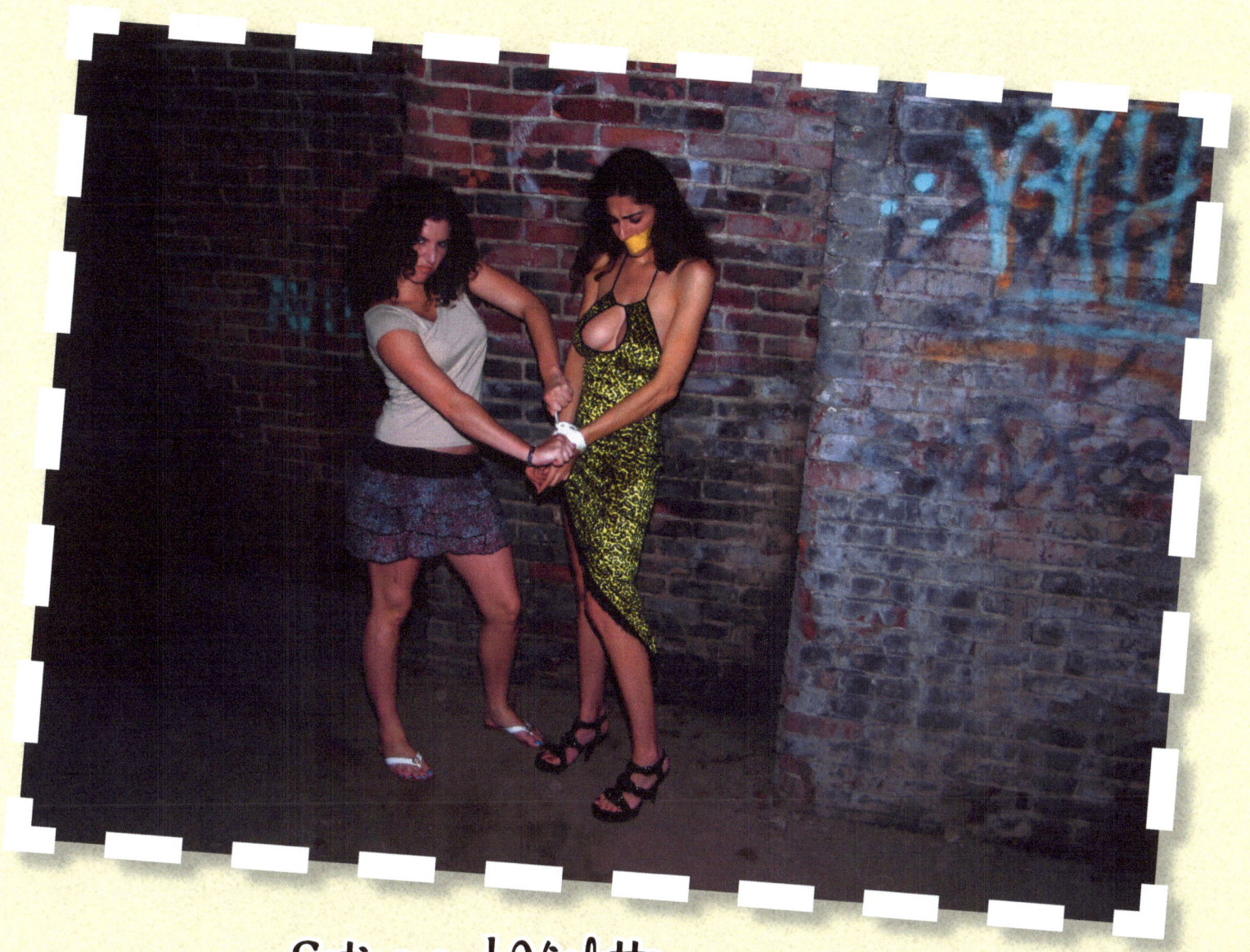

Sativa and Violetta

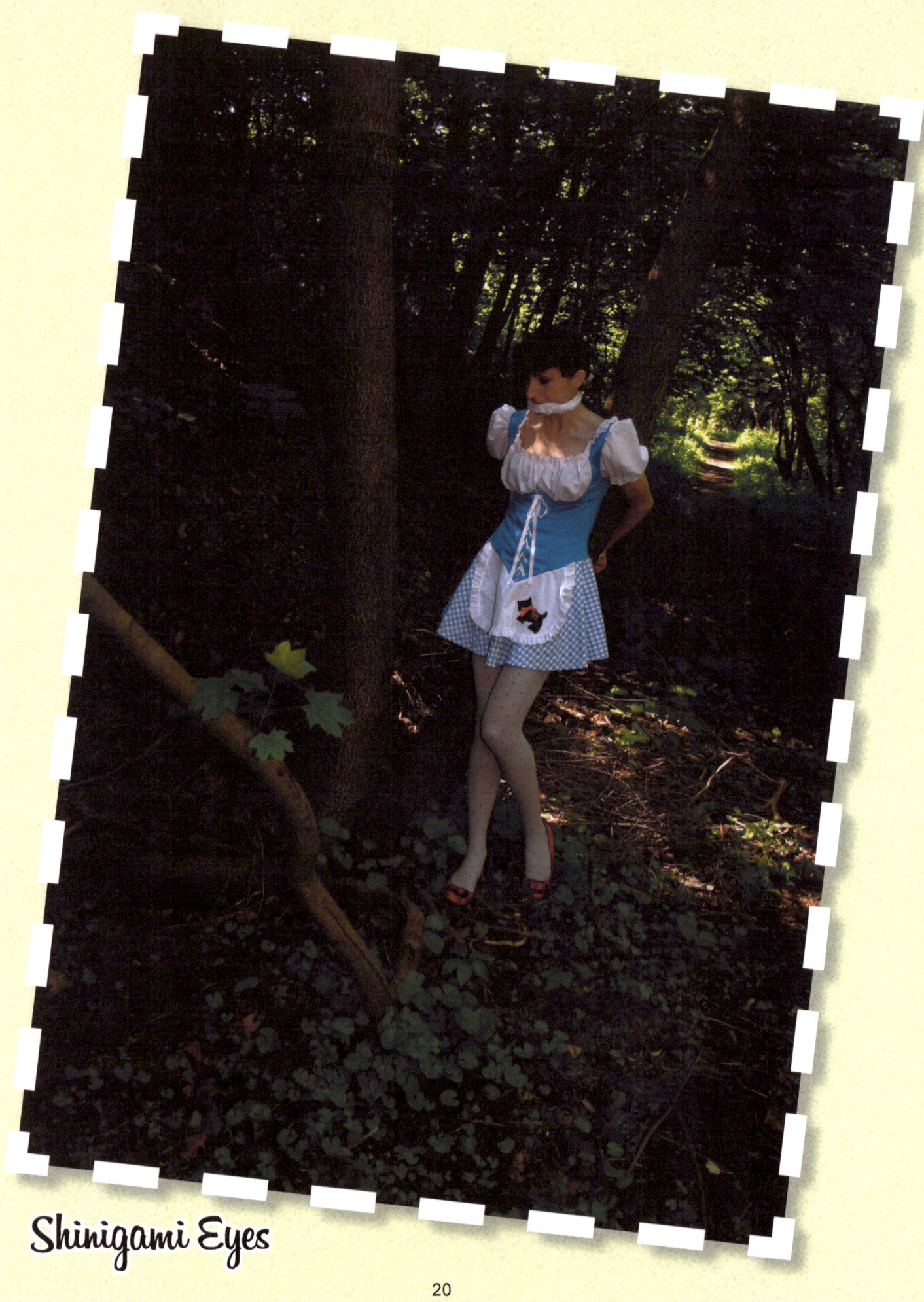

Shinigami Eyes

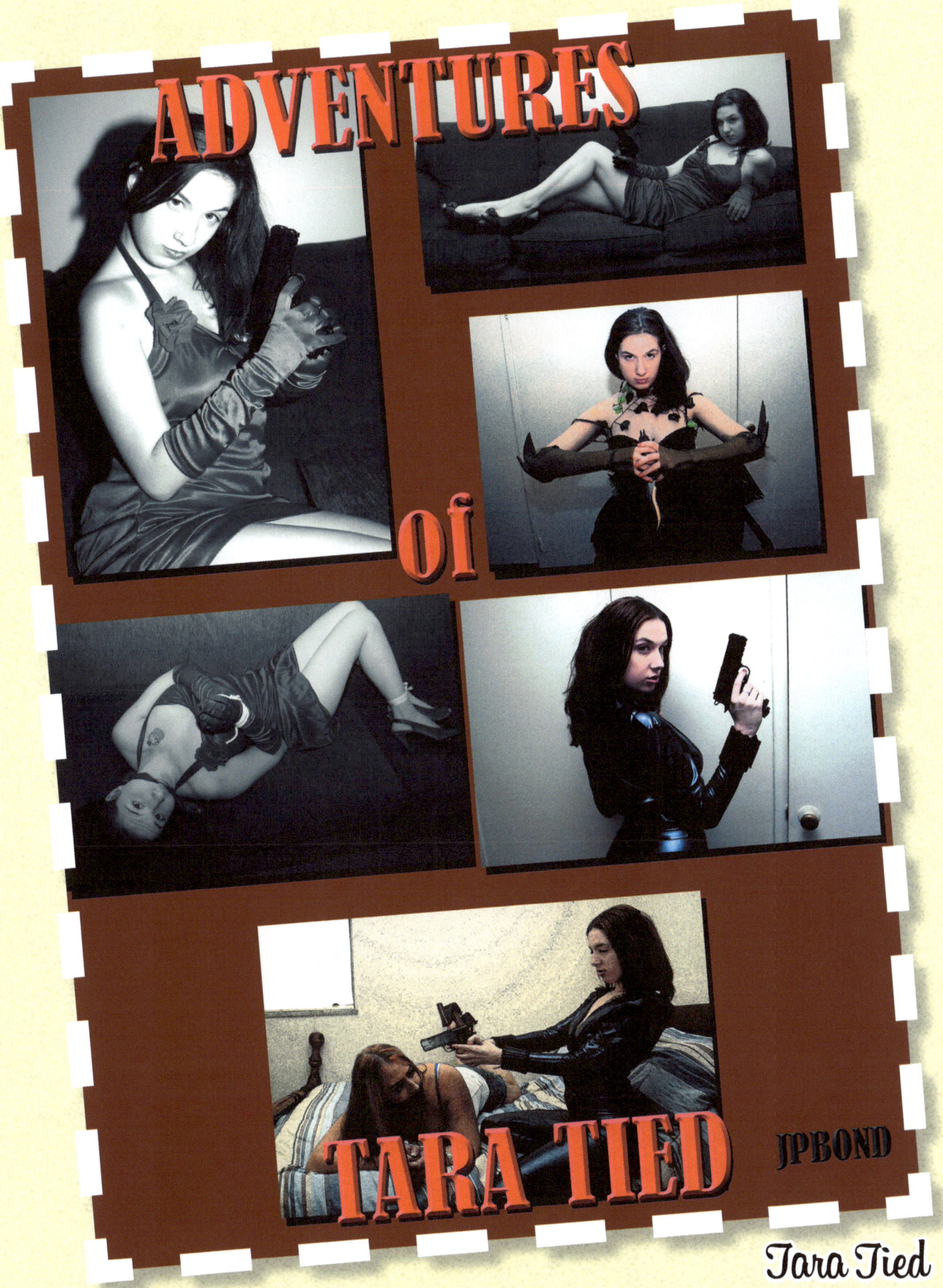

ADVENTURES of TARA TIED

JPBOND

Tara Tied

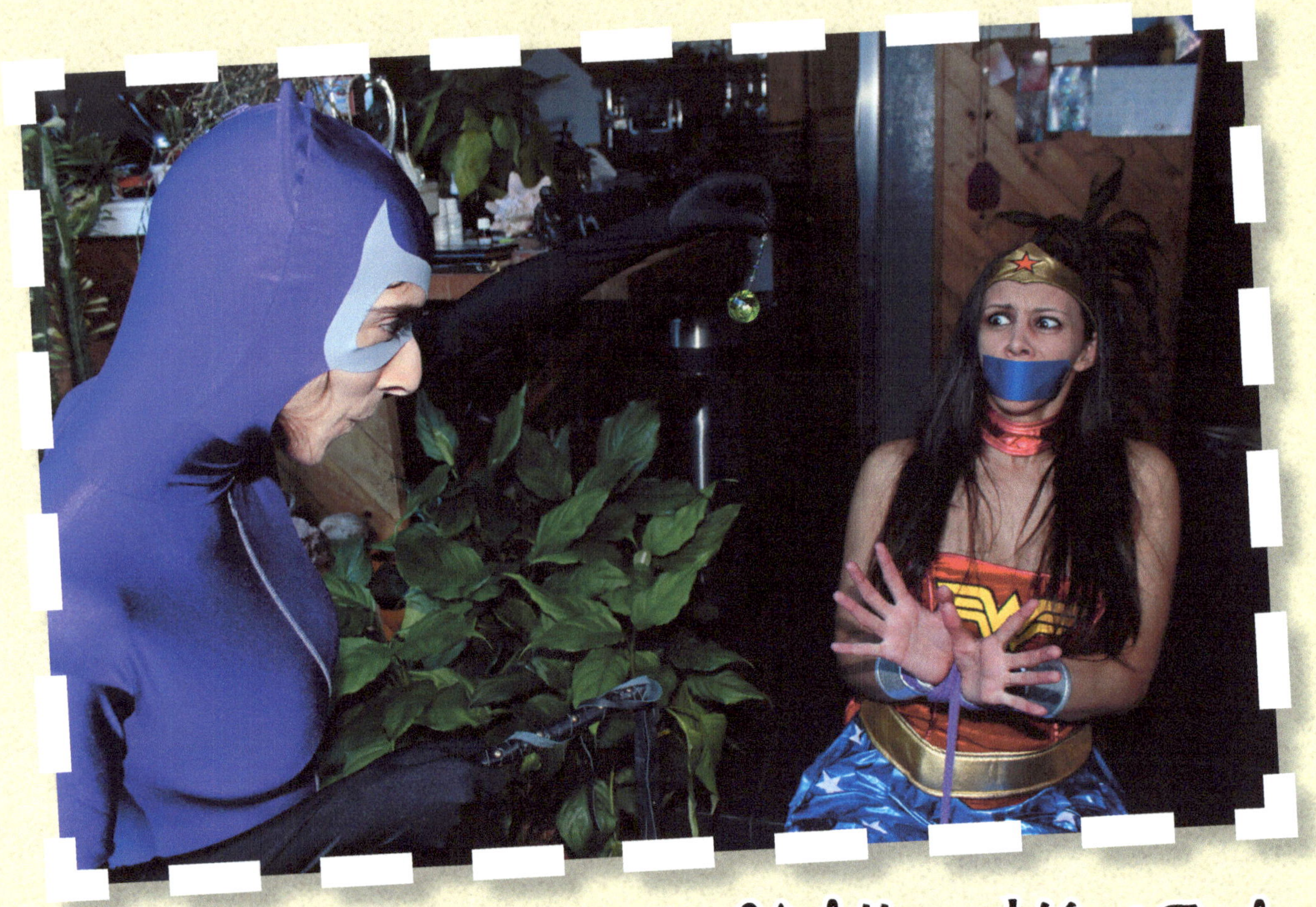

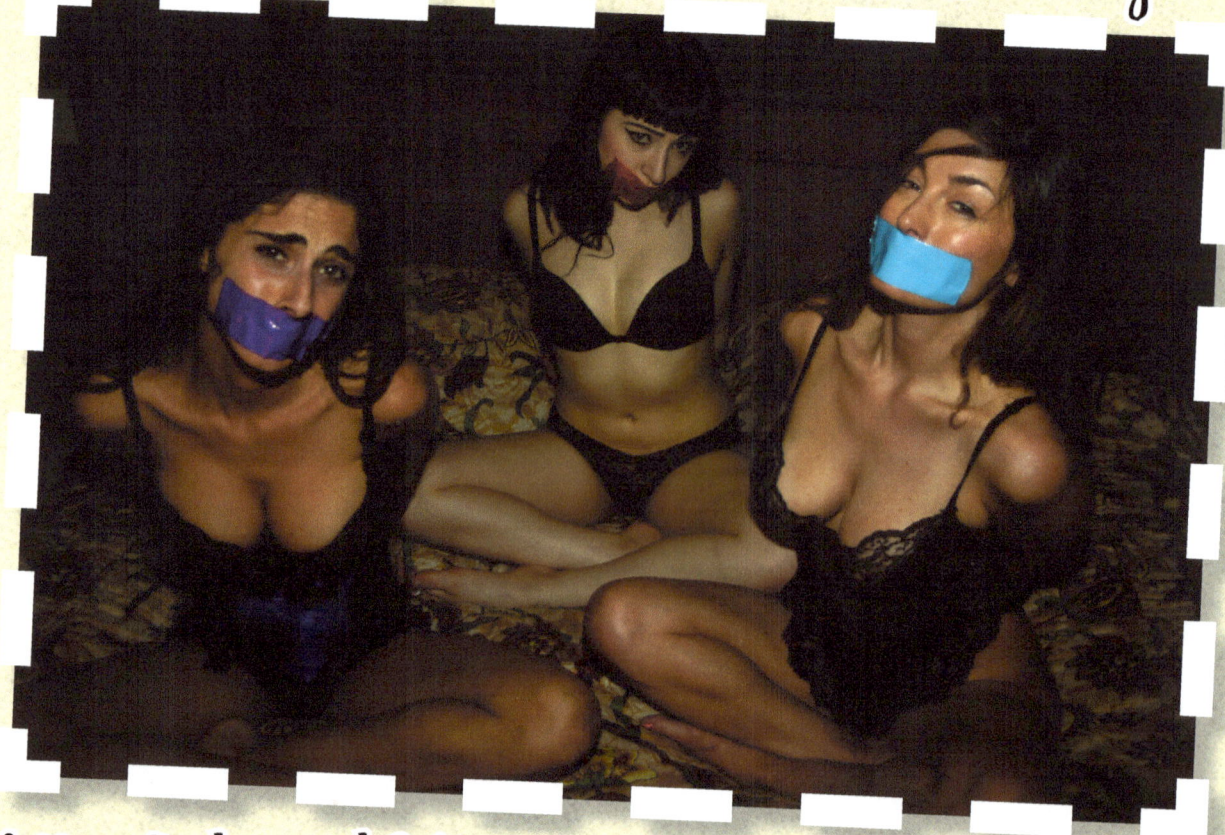

Violetta and Kerri Taylor

Violetta, Lydia and Mia

22

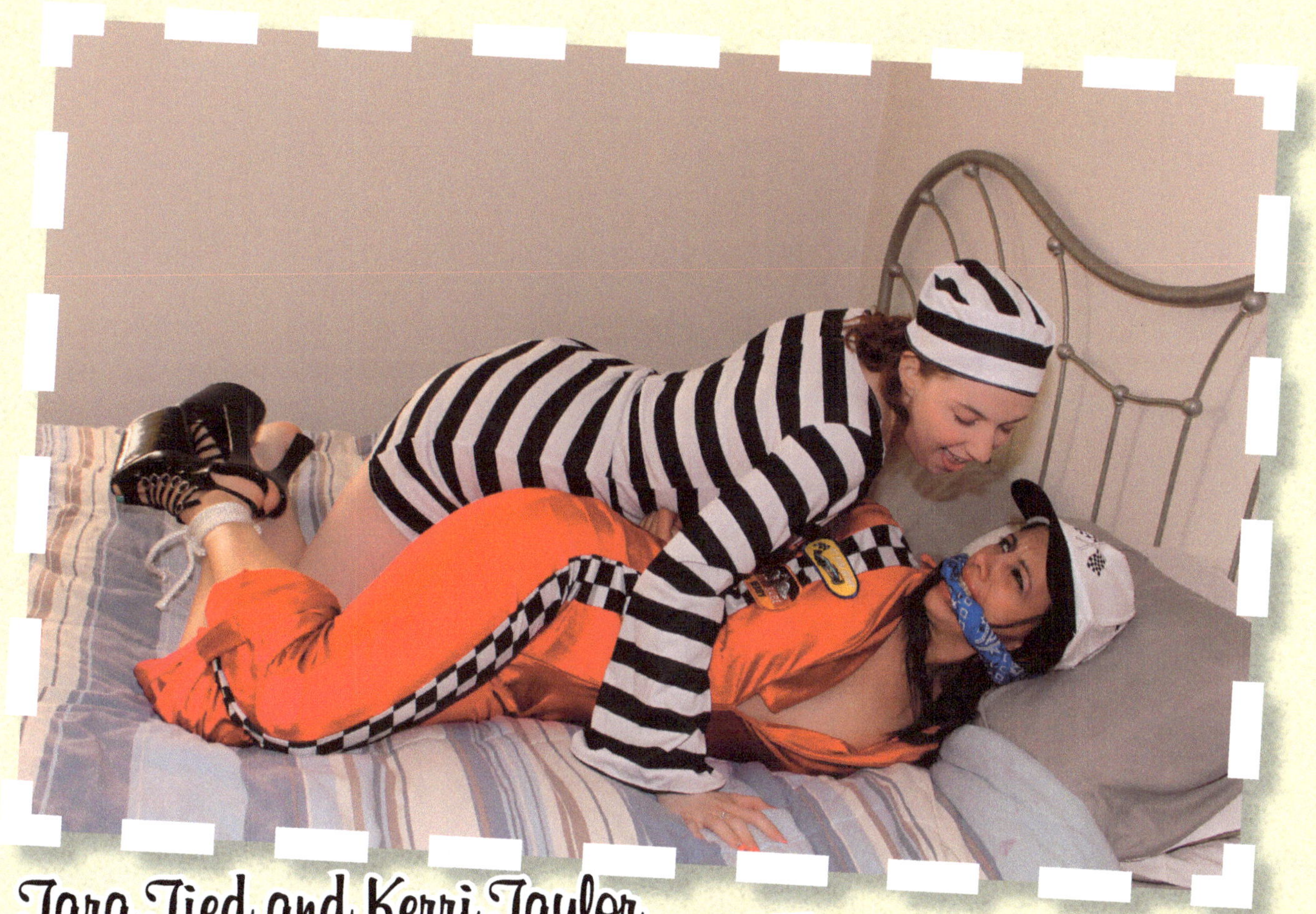

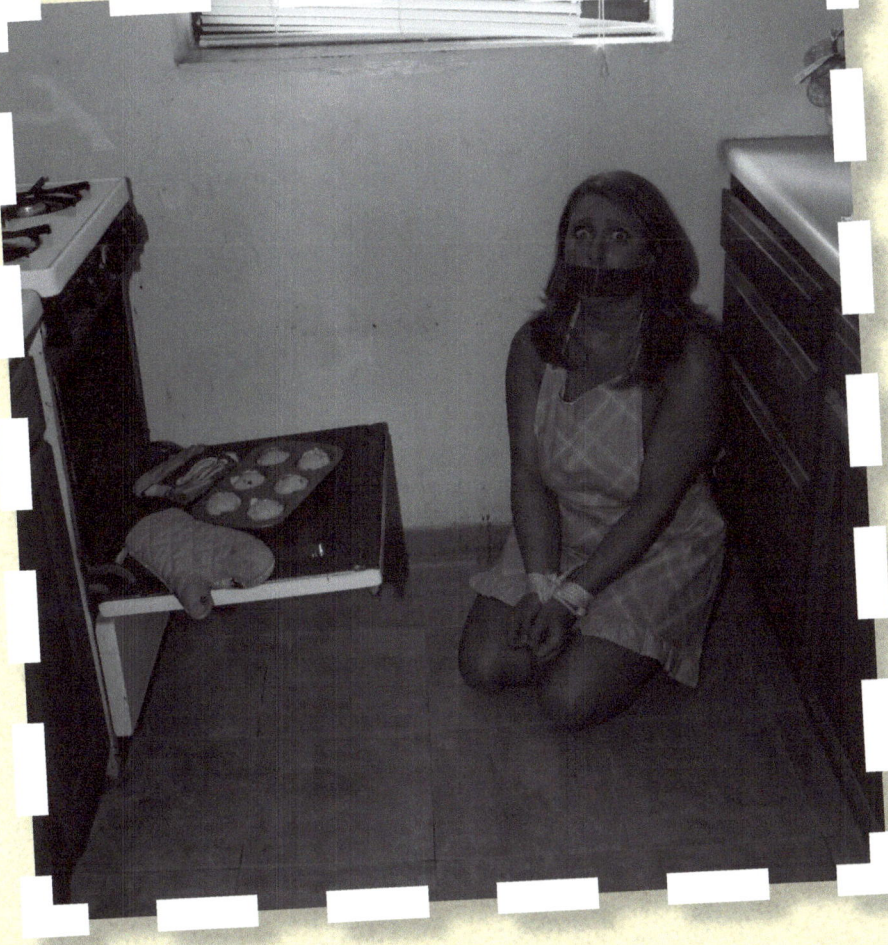

Tara Tied and Kerri Taylor

Anastasia